SCOTTISH CASTLES

PHOTOGRAPHS BY
COLIN BAXTER

SCOTTISH CASTLES

Castles are compelling features in Scotland's landscape. For more than five centuries, Scots built them, lived and died in them, attacked and defended them. To visit them today is to come face to face with the nation's turbulent past.

Scotland has over 2,000 castles. A select few were the mighty strongholds of the ruling royal dynasties – the Canmores, Bruces and Stewarts; others were the domains of the leading barons in the realm. The majority, however, were built as fortified residences for lairds (lords) much lower down the social ladder.

Castles were introduced into Scotland around 1100, not only by the Canmores, but also by the descendants of the Vikings, for Scotland was then a divided land. Most early castles were motte-and-baileys, built of earth and timber. But in the 13th century mighty stone strongholds appeared. Many were badly damaged during the bloody Wars of Independence with England (1296-1356), and when that conflict ended, some of the old baronial families, such as the Balliols and Comyns, had been wiped out and replaced by new dynasties: the Douglases, Campbells and the rest. These new lords introduced a new type of castle, focused on a lofty tower house. Scottish lairds continued their love-affair with the tower-house castle until well into the 17th century.

Despite their associations with the landholding class, castles were central to the lives of many Scots, no matter their status. Castles were where they worked and worshipped, partied and paid their rents, were imprisoned and punished. Castles were not simply lordly residences; they served as guest houses, army barracks, estate offices and law courts too.

Today, only a few castles continue to serve as noble residences. Most have been abandoned long since. But their gaunt, forbidding ruined shells still have the power to fill those who gaze upon them with awe and wonder – just as they did all those centuries ago.

CASTLE STALKER, Argyll – built on *Eilean an Stalcaire* by the Stewarts of Appin in the early 16th century.

KILCHURN CASTLE, Loch Awe, Argyll (left) – the 15th-century seat of the Campbells of Glenorchy.

BALVENIE CASTLE, Moray – the mighty 13th-century stronghold of the 'Red' Comyns, the Earls of Buchan.

CASTLE CAMPBELL, Clackmannan (right) – the Lowland residence of the Campbell Earls of Argyll.

EDINBURGH CASTLE, City of Edinburgh – Scotland's premier royal castle has dominated
the capital city with majesty for centuries. It remains a vibrant part of national life, no time
more so than when the castle esplanade hosts the EDINBURGH MILITARY TATTOO (left).

DUNNOTTAR CASTLE,
Aberdeenshire (right) –
the stronghold of the Keiths, Earls
Marischal of Scotland, clinging to
its nearly inaccessible promontory
jutting into the North Sea. The
Honours of Scotland, the nation's
Crown Jewels, lay hidden here over
the winter of 1651-2 during Oliver
Cromwell's invasion of Scotland.

SPYNIE PALACE, Moray (left) – the
fortified residence of the Bishops
of Moray from the 13th century to
the Reformation in 1560, and the
most complete medieval episcopal
palace surviving in Scotland. The
huge 'David's Tower', built about
1470, was the largest Scottish
tower house ever built.

CRAIGIEVAR CASTLE, Aberdeenshire (left) – is one of the last tower houses built in Scotland. Completed in 1625 by William Forbes, nicknamed 'Danzig Willie', who made his money in business with the Baltic states. The Forbes family lived here for almost 350 years, before gifting the property to the National Trust for Scotland.

ST ANDREWS CASTLE, Fife (right) – the episcopal palace of St Andrews suffered greatly during the struggle leading up to the Reformation of 1560. George Wishart, Protestant preacher, was burnt as a heretic in front of its walls, and Cardinal Beaton's bloodied corpse was hung from the battlements.

BALMORAL CASTLE, Royal Deeside (left) and HUNTLY CASTLE, Aberdeenshire (above).

LOCHRANZA CASTLE, North Ayrshire (above) and BALLINDALLOCH CASTLE, Moray (right).

GLAMIS CASTLE, Angus (left) and CAWDOR CASTLE, Highland (above) –
two ancient and noble seats both with literary links courtesy of Shakespeare
and MacBeth (1040-57) but with no tangible associations in history.

HERMITAGE CASTLE, Scottish Borders – a forbidding ruin of the Black Douglases, in deepest Liddesdale.

INVERARAY CASTLE, Argyll (right) – built about 1750 as the seat of the Campbells, Dukes of Argyll.

DUNVEGAN CASTLE, Isle of Skye (left) and INVERNESS CASTLE, Highland (above).

CRATHES CASTLE, Kincardineshire (above) and Corgarff Castle, Aberdeenshire (right).

URQUHART CASTLE, Loch Ness (left) – the sprawling royal stronghold majestically sited on a promontory on the shore of Loch Ness. The fortress figured prominently in the bitter Wars of Independence with England, and in the long struggle between the Scottish Crown and the MacDonalds, Lords of the Isles, that followed.

EILEAN DONAN CASTLE, West Highlands (right) – an eye-catching spectacle on the banks of Loch Duich. The castle that today rises up from the rocky 'island of St Donan' is largely an early 20th-century restoration of the original stronghold of the Mackenzies of Kintail and later the MacRaes, blown up during the 1719 Jacobite Rising.

ARDVRECK CASTLE, Highland – the Marquis of Montrose was captured here in 1650.

BLAIR CASTLE, Perthshire (left) – the ancestral seat of the Murrays, Dukes of Atholl.

DUART CASTLE, Argyll (above) and CAERLAVEROCK CASTLE, Dumfries & Galloway (right) – two mighty 13th-century curtain-walled castles. Duart was the chief seat of the MacLeans, whilst Caerlaverock was the domain of the Maxwells.

STIRLING CASTLE, Stirling – one of Scotland's great medieval royal castles.

Published in Great Britain in 2007 by Colin Baxter Photography Ltd,
Grantown-on-Spey, Moray PH26 3NA, Scotland
www.colinbaxter.co.uk

Photographs © Colin Baxter 2007
Text by Chris Tabraham
Copyright © Colin Baxter Photography Ltd 2007
All rights reserved.

No part of this book may be reproduced,
stored in a retrieval system or transmitted in any form or
by any means without prior written permission of the publishers.

A CIP Catalogue record for this book is available
from the British Library.

ISBN 978-1-84107-362-0   Printed in China

Page one photograph: FYVIE CASTLE, Aberdeenshire
Page two photograph: URQUHART CASTLE, Loch Ness, Highland
Front cover photograph: CASTLE STALKER, Argyll
Back cover photograph: EDINBURGH CASTLE